CHIMPANZ

Written and edited by **Barbara Taylor Cork**

Consultant Miranda Stevenson BA PhD
Curator of Animals, Royal Zoological Society of Scotland

JUMP!

Two-Can Publishing Ltd

First published in Great Britain in 1989 by
Two-Can Publishing Ltd
27 Cowper Street
London EC2A 4AP

© Two-Can Publishing Ltd., 1989

Text by Barbara Taylor Cork
Design by David Bennett
Printed and bound by Purnells, England

British Library Cataloguing in Publication Data

Chimpanzees.
    I. Chimpanzees — For children
    599.88'44

    ISBN 1-85434-085-9

Photograph Credits:
p.4 Bruce Coleman/Helmut Albrecht p.5 Bruce Coleman/R. Williams p.6 (top) Bruce Coleman/Helmut Albrecht (bottom) Bruce Coleman/J. Mackinnon
p.7 (left) Bruce Coleman/Peter Jackson (right) Bruce Coleman/Peter Davey p.8 Bruce Coleman/Helmut Albrecht p.9 Zefa p.10 Bruce Coleman/Helmut Albrecht
p.11 Bruce Coleman/Helmut Albrecht p.12 (left) Bruce Coleman/Peter Davey (right) NHPA/S Robinson p.14 Ardea/Jean-Paul Ferrero p.15 Ardea/Kenneth W. Fink
p.16 (left) Bruce Coleman/Helmut Albrecht (right) Bruce Coleman/Peter Davey p.17 (top) Ardea/Kenneth W. Fink (bottom) Ardea/Yann Arthus-Bernard
Cover Photo: Bruce Coleman/R. Williams

Illustration Credits:
p.1 Malcolm Livingstone p.3 Malcolm Livingstone/Alan Rogers p.4 Malcolm Livingstone p.9 Malcolm Livingstone p.11 Malcolm Livingstone
p.13 Malcolm Livingstone p.15 Malcolm Livingstone p.18-19 Alastair Graham p.20-24 Tor Morisse p.25 Alan Rogers p.27 Claire Legemah p.28-29 Malcolm
Livingstone p.30 Tony Wells p.31 Alan Rogers p.32 Malcolm Livingstone

CONTENTS

LOOKING AT CHIMPANZEES

Chimpanzees are intelligent, noisy animals that live in the forests of West and Central Africa. They look and behave like us in many ways and are probably our closest living relative.

Because chimpanzees are very clever, they can solve problems and make and use simple tools. They use stones as hammers and chew plants to make sponges. Chimpanzees are quick to copy and learn things; some chimpanzees have even been taught the sort of sign language used by deaf people.

Did you know that chimpanzees are not monkeys? They are a kind of ape. Apes do not have a tail and their arms are longer than their legs. Male chimpanzees grow up to 1.5 metres (5 feet) tall and are bigger than the females.

▲ A chimpanzee has long, thick black hair all over its body except on its face, hands and feet. Older chimpanzees grow long, white hairs on the face and chest.

► Like us, chimpanzees have good eyesight and can see in colour. Their sense of hearing is important, especially for communicating with each other.

CHIMPANZEE FACTS

Unlike monkeys, chimpanzees don't have a tail.

An adult male chimpanzee is three or four times stronger than a person of the same height and weight.

The closest relatives of the chimpanzee are the two other great apes, the gorilla and the orang-utan.

LIFE IN THE FOREST

Chimpanzees live mainly in thick forests where it is warm all year round and day and night are the same length. For about half the year, it hardly ever rains. This is called the dry season. For the rest of the year, it rains on most days. This is called the wet season.

When it rains, a chimpanzee usually sits hunched up with its arms around its knees and its head down. Chimpanzees don't shelter from the rain and so get soaking wet.

At the start of a heavy storm, some male chimpanzees may do a wild 'rain dance'. They charge about waving branches and making a lot of noise. No one is sure why they do this.

▲ In the middle of the day, chimpanzees usually rest for a while in the trees or on the ground.

▲ When it rains, a mother chimpanzee may try to keep her baby dry.

▶ Chimpanzees can bring their big toe across to touch their other toes. This helps them to keep a firm grip on branches as they climb through the trees.

▼ Chimpanzees can stand upright and walk for short distances on two legs. This chimpanzee is carrying a baobab fruit.

Even though chimpanzees are often very noisy, they can also be quiet when they don't want to be found.

Chimpanzees spend some time on the ground and some time in the trees. They are very good at climbing. To go up a tree trunk, a chimpanzee may put its arms round the trunk and walk up the tree with its legs. To move about in the trees, chimpanzees swing from branch to branch using one hand at a time.

On the ground, chimpanzees usually walk on all fours. They keep their feet flat on the ground to take their weight but curl up their fingers so that they walk on their knuckles.

LIVING IN A GROUP

▲ When chimpanzees groom each other, they huddle close together and carefully search through the fur with their fingers. They often don't find anything, but grooming feels pleasant and helps the chimpanzees to relax.

Chimpanzees like to live with other chimpanzees in a group, which is called a community. Small communities of about 4-8 chimpanzees move around together but they may sometimes meet up with other communities to form larger gatherings of 20-80 chimpanzees.

Males tend to stay in one community and may spend a lot of time with special male friends in their group. Young females move about from one community to another. Once a female has a family, she spends most of her time with her youngsters, although she meets up with other chimpanzees from time to time.

The chimpanzees in a community spend a lot of time touching each other. They may hug and kiss each other and pat each other on the back. They also pick through each others fur to get rid of dry skin, dirt and small insects. This is called grooming. It helps the chimpanzees to stay clean and healthy but it also comforts them and is a way of saying "I want to be friends".

Each chimpanzee has its own place in the community. Some of the chimpanzees are less important than others. When they meet a more important chimpanzee, they crouch down to show their respect. The important chimpanzee may reach out to pat them. This is a way of saying "I will not attack you at the moment". The less important chimpanzees also groom the more important chimpanzees as a sign of respect.

The male chimpanzees defend the community from enemies, such as baboons and leopards. One of the males is the leader. Every so often, he rushes about, stamping on the ground, dragging branches and making a lot of noise. As he does this, his hair stands on end, which makes him look bigger and more frightening. This shows the other chimpanzees that he is big and strong enough to be the top chimpanzee and defend the group. The leader eats first and the other chimpanzees give way to him and let him do as he pleases.

From time to time, other male chimpanzees challenge the top chimpanzee and try to take over as the leader. To help him keep his position, the leader relies on his experience and intelligence as well as his special friends in the group.

▼ One chimpanzee may hug another chimpanzee to comfort it and show that they are friends.

CHIEF CHIMPANZEES

Can you tell which one of these chimpanzees is more important?

MAKING A NEST

Every night, a chimpanzee makes a nest to sleep in. The nest is usually more than 2 metres (6 feet) up in the trees where the chimpanzee will be safer from enemies. The chimpanzee chooses a firm base, such as a fork in the branches, and bends over a few leafy twigs. It stands on the ends of the twigs to hold them in place and tucks in a few more leaves around the edge to make a springy platform. Sometimes, the chimpanzee picks a bunch of leaves to use as a pillow. It takes about five minutes for a chimpanzee to build a nest.

Chimpanzees usually stay in their nests throughout the night. They do not sleep all this time but it is safer in a nest than in the dark forest. When it is raining, the chimpanzees often don't want to get up in the morning. In the wet season, the ground is usually damp and a chimpanzee may make a simple daytime nest to rest in. This nest may be on the ground or in the trees.

▼ A very young chimpanzee sleeps in its mother's nest. Each adult chimpanzee makes a nest of its own. Baby chimpanzees learn how to make a nest by watching their mother and practising on their own.

TALKING

Chimpanzees use a lot of different sounds to 'talk' to each other. If chimpanzees feel safe and happy, they grunt quietly to each other. They often make these noises during grooming or feeding. When chimpanzees find a good place to feed, they often get excited and make loud barking or hooting noises. If they are angry or afraid, they scream loudly.

If one group of chimpanzees meets another, both groups leap about and scream at each other. The adult males may charge at the other group. They do all this to tell the other chimpanzees "We live in this place, keep out".

▲ This chimpanzee is pouting to show that it wants something, such as food. What sort of sound do you think it is making?

CHIMPANZEE FACES

Angry face — lips shut tight, hair on end

Excited or frightened face — mouth open, top and bottom teeth showing

Pout face — lips pushed forward when chimpanzee want's something

Play face — bottom teeth showing

SEARCHING FOR FOOD

To search for food, chimpanzees usually split up into small groups. Most of their food is not very nutritious, so they have to eat a lot to get the goodness they need. Chimpanzees spend about 8 hours a day finding food.

Chimpanzees are mainly vegetarians and eat a lot of fruit. When there is a lot of ripe fruit on a tree, many of the chimpanzees in a community gather together to join in the feast. From time to time, chimpanzees also feed on leaves, bark, termites, ants, honey and birds' eggs.

To reach inside the mounds of soil where termites live, a chimpanzee makes a small hole

▲ This chimpanzee is using a stick as a tool to dig for food in the ground. Chimpanzees may also use sticks to reach the honey in a bees' nest.

▲ Chimpanzees sometimes eat soil which contains salt and other minerals. This helps them to stay healthy.

FOOD FACTS

Chimpanzees don't drink very much because there is a lot of water in the food they eat. But they may crumple up some leaves to soak up water for drinking.

An adult chimpanzee can eat up to 50 bananas in one meal.

A chimpanzee may spend 3 hours or more 'fishing' for termites. Most 'fishing' is carried out by females and their young.

with its fingers. Then it breaks off a leafy twig, peels off the leaves and pokes the twig into the hole. When the chimpanzee pulls out the twig, it licks off the termites clinging to the end. Termites nest in the same place for years so chimpanzees return to the same nest year after year. Young chimpanzees learn how to 'fish' for termites by watching their mother. Most termite 'fishing' is done by females and their young.

On rare occasions, chimpanzees will attack and kill small animals, such as monkeys or baby pigs. The males usually do the hunting and may use sticks and stones as weapons. Several males may help each other to kill the animal. If other chimpanzees in the community hold out their hands, the males may share some of the meat with them.

BABY CHIMPANZEES

A female chimpanzee is old enough to have her first baby when she is about 12 years old. She usually has one baby at a time. Chimpanzees have babies only once every four or five years so the other chimpanzees in a community are always fascinated by a new arrival.

The newborn chimpanzee is tiny and has very little hair. It is helpless at first and cannot do anything except suck its mother's milk and cling to her fur with its tiny fists. When its mother moves about, the baby clings underneath her body.

◄ Young chimpanzees may ride on their mother's back for several years.

When the baby is about two months old, it starts to take an interest in nearby objects. At three months, the baby can climb about over its mother's body and starts to touch everything within reach. The mother spends a lot of time playing with her baby. At this stage, the baby's teeth begin to come through.

When the baby is about five months old, it begins to ride on its mother's back. At first the baby keeps slipping off but it soon learns how to cling on without falling off. When its mother rests, the baby slides off her back and explores its surroundings. The mother keeps a close watch on her baby and is always ready to help if it gets into trouble.

BABY FACTS

When it is born, a baby chimpanzee weighs about 0.9-1.8 kilograms (2-4 pounds) — less than half as much as a human baby.

Very young babies are carried underneath their mother.

▲ A baby chimpanzee drinks its mother's milk for about five years but starts to try out solid foods when it is about four months old.

GROWING UP

When it is eight months old, the baby chimpanzee makes its first attempt at building a nest and starts to play games with its brothers and sisters. The games help the young chimpanzees to learn how to look after themselves.

When it is a year old, the young chimpanzee starts to take part in the life of the group. It has to learn how to behave with the other chimpanzees and how to groom them in the correct way. It soon finds out that a young chimpanzee gives way to older chimpanzees. But if its mother is an important chimpanzee, the youngster will also have an important position in the group.

By now it will have started to build its own nest and sleep separately from its mother. Even if its mother has another baby, the young chimpanzee can still run to her for comfort and protection. When the young chimpanzees are about 6 years old, they may start to move around without their mothers for a short time. They still have a lot to learn. A male chimpanzee will not be fully mature until he is about 15 years old and a female will not start a family of her own until she is about 12 years old. A chimpanzee may live 40 years or more.

▲ A mother chimpanzee spends six years or more looking after her youngster. If its mother dies, a young chimpanzee may not survive.

▲ This young chimpanzee is learning how to use a tool. As they grow up, chimpanzees have to learn many skills.

SAVE THE CHIMPANZEE

▲ Only a few thousand pygmy chimpanzees are left in the wild. They live in Central Africa.

▼ These zoo-bred chimpanzees are being taught how to survive in the wild before they are set free in the forest.

About 50,000-200,000 chimpanzees live in Africa, but in some West African countries there are only a few hundred left.

The biggest problem facing the chimpanzee is lack of space. People are constantly cutting down the forests to make way for villages and farmland so there is less room for the chimpanzees to live. In some places, chimpanzees are hunted for food. Chimpanzees are also used in research into human diseases.

More still needs to be done to protect the rain forests where the chimpanzees live and make sure they survive in the future.

CHIMPANZEE GAME

Can you help the photographer to find her way back to her camp?

To play this game, you will need a dice and some counters.

If you land on a black square, go forward one square. If you land on a pink square go back one square.

START

Throw one to start.

Chimpanzees don't see you hiding in tree. Go forward 1 square.

You get lost in the rain. Go back 1 square.

You lose map
of forest.
Go back
to start.

Stop to watch
chimpanzees
grooming.
Miss a turn.

See smoke
from campfire.
Go forward
2 squares.

FINISH

Well done!
You've reached
the camp.